Fish Hotel

Written by Lynn Markham & Illustrated by Justin Sipiorski

Text copyright © 2016 Center for Land Use Education
University of Wisconsin-Extension
Illustrations copyright © 2016 Justin Sipiorski
Layout and graphic design by Elizabeth Rossi, University of Wisconsin, Environmental Resources Center
Edited by Kelly Dwyer, Dan Menzel and Mary Sipiorski

First edition – 2016
ISBN-10: 0-692-69665-2
ISBN-13: 978-0-692-69665-1

Library of Congress cataloging
Markham, Lynn
Fish Hotel / by Lynn Markham
PZ7.M339458 Fi 2016

Summary: Two cousins discover an underwater oasis where fish and aquatic creatures enjoy the benefits of trees in lakes, which are 'fish hotels'. Then they take action to help the fish.
1. Trees – Ecology – Juvenile fiction. 2. Fishes – Habitat – Juvenile fiction. 3. Nature stories.

We gratefully acknowledge the funding provided for this undertaking by the Wisconsin Department of Natural Resources, University of Wisconsin-Extension and the Wisconsin Environmental Education Board. We thank the following friends and colleagues for helping us with their ideas and expertise: Carol LeBreck – Bony Lake; Scott Toshner, Greg Sass, Pam Toshner, Dale Rezabek, Michael Wenholz, Kay Lutze, and Heidi Bunk – Wisconsin Department of Natural Resources; Justin VanDeHey, Jonathan Stoffregen, Danielle Rupp, James Cook, Bob Bell, Bill Fisher, and Nancy Turyk – University of Wisconsin–Stevens Point; Amy Kowalski – University of Wisconsin-Extension Lakes; Kyle Magyera – Wisconsin Wetlands Association; Nicole Ozanich – Portage County Public Library; Amy Kelsey, Susan Tesarik, Heidi Kennedy, Tessa Bruckhart and Tate Bruckhart.

Please direct comments or inquiries about copyright permission to:
Center for Land Use Education
College of Natural Resources, UWSP
800 Reserve St., Stevens Point, WI 54481
715.346.3879
landcenter@uwsp.edu

Illustration scanning by Arthur H. Robinson Map Library, University of Wisconsin-Madison

DNR Publication WT-1003 2016   UWEX Publication GWQ071 2016

For Tessa, Tate and Dan for being my family and lake buddies. And for all of the waterfront property owners who share their shorelines with the fish. – Lynn

For Emily, Sophie and Hugo. – Justin

For as long as she could remember, Tessa had loved fish. When she went canoeing with her family, she spent the whole time leaning over the edge of the canoe watching the fish.

During the second week of summer vacation, Tessa and her family went to their shared family cottage on Lake Katherine. She was so excited to spend a whole week playing with her cousin Hugo and watching fish at the lake! Hugo had promised to teach her how to snorkel, and she had been practicing in the bathtub at home.

It was dark when they arrived at the cottage. Uncle Henry greeted them and helped them with their bags. Tessa shared an upstairs bedroom with Hugo, who had arrived with his parents a couple of days earlier. The two cousins stayed up late that night whispering excitedly about all of their plans.

5

The next morning Tessa and Hugo woke up early and ran down to the lake together.

Hugo helped Tessa put on her mask. The two of them sank down into the water grinning at each other.

"Whoa! It's a completely new world underwater," said Tessa.

"Yeah, there are so many new things to see," replied Hugo.

They both laughed at the funny sound of their voices coming up through their snorkels.

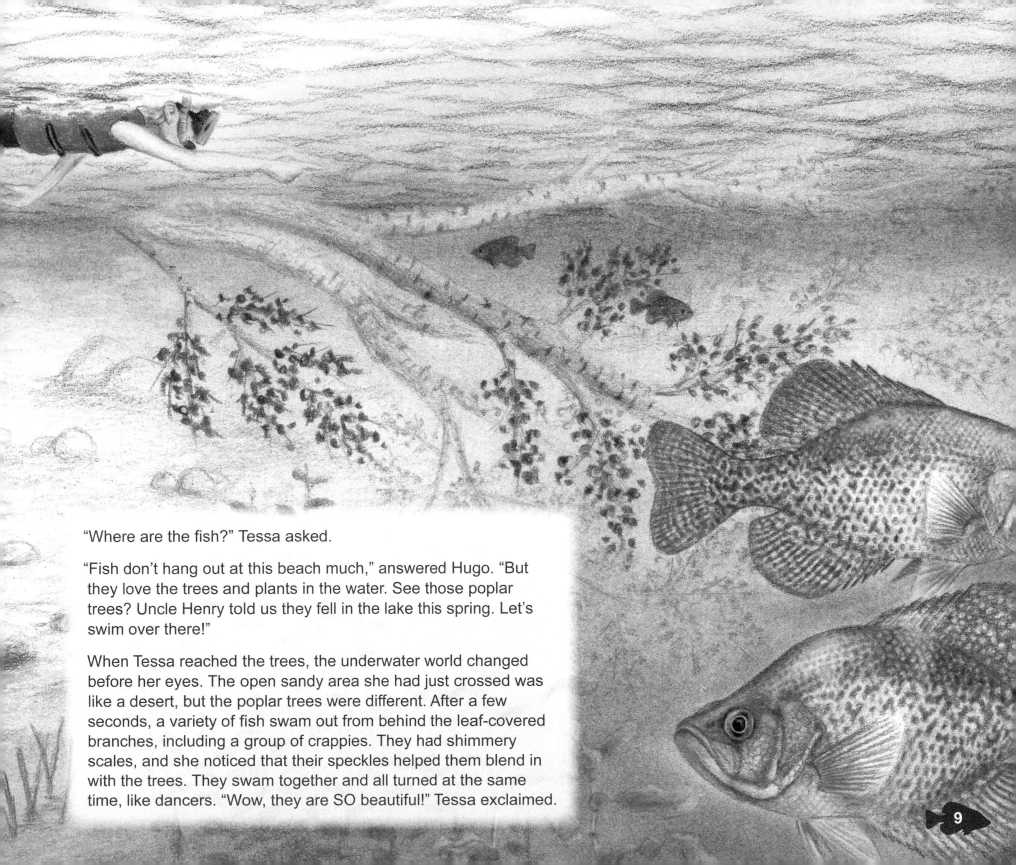

"Where are the fish?" Tessa asked.

"Fish don't hang out at this beach much," answered Hugo. "But they love the trees and plants in the water. See those poplar trees? Uncle Henry told us they fell in the lake this spring. Let's swim over there!"

When Tessa reached the trees, the underwater world changed before her eyes. The open sandy area she had just crossed was like a desert, but the poplar trees were different. After a few seconds, a variety of fish swam out from behind the leaf-covered branches, including a group of crappies. They had shimmery scales, and she noticed that their speckles helped them blend in with the trees. They swam together and all turned at the same time, like dancers. "Wow, they are SO beautiful!" Tessa exclaimed.

Then Tessa saw some minnows she hadn't noticed before because they blended in with the leaves. One minnow grabbed an insect off a leaf and munched it down – lunch, thanks to the tree. Tessa pointed and Hugo nodded, smiling.

Suddenly the minnows darted behind the leaves. Tessa looked behind her and saw a largemouth bass swimming toward her. The bass stopped and stared at Tessa for a few long seconds, as if he wanted to tell her something. Then he slowly turned and swam away.

"Wow! Did you see that largemouth bass?" asked Tessa.

"It was huge! And did you see those minnows swim away from it?" asked Hugo.

"Yeah, the minnows and little fish really need that tree for safety so the big fish can't eat them for lunch!" exclaimed Tessa.

"I know," said Hugo. "That tree is their home – a safe place for them."

"Are there enough trees in the lake so all the little fish can find shelter?" asked Tessa.

"I don't know," said Hugo. "Let's see how many trees we can find in other parts of the lake."

As they climbed out of the water, Tessa noticed a spot along the shoreline where there was a slit in the ground where she could see right down to the tree roots. Tessa and Hugo peered down into the slit and saw the lake bottom, which was covered with roots, leaves, and small rocks.

"Hey, look at that red eye!" said Hugo.

Tessa looked closer and saw an olive-brown fish lurking among the roots.

All of a sudden, a brilliantly colored fish flashed through the slit and then disappeared into a nearby bed of water plants.

On their quest to find out if there were enough trees in the lake for all of the fish, Tessa and Hugo snorkeled over to a cluster of trees that included a gigantic white pine tree. The white pine looked very different than the fallen poplar trees they had snorkeled by earlier; most of its needles and small branches were gone. They were standing in shallow water when they noticed a woman wading on the other side of the trees. Hugo waved.

The woman, with a twinkle in her eye, said, "Hi, kids! Are you checking out our trees?"

"Hi, Carol! This is my cousin Tessa. Yes, we're looking for fish."

"Welcome, Tessa! Well, you kids have come to the right place. The fish love these trees! Do you know the story of this white pine?"

Hugo and Tessa shook their heads.

"This tree grew taller than a ten-story building. My dad climbed it as a kid each summer to peek into the eagle's nest near the top to see if there were any chicks, and to get an awesome view of the lake. Ten years ago, a big windstorm blew so hard that the tree crashed down into the lake. It was over two hundred years old! When this majestic tree fell, we heard a giant WHOMP and felt the cottage shake."

Tessa looked down at the trunk of the tree, as wide as a refrigerator, and tried to imagine that noise.

"After being a home to eagles, squirrels, woodpeckers and other animals for over two hundred years standing up, it started a second life…in the lake. My dad told me that there used to be a lot more trees in the lake, and the fishing was much better then. So I left this tree in the water to become an underwater home for fish – a fish hotel."

Tessa and Hugo smiled, imagining an underwater hotel with guest rooms and a restaurant.

"But what happened to all of its needles?" Tessa asked.

"In the first few years the tree was in the lake, the needles and twigs fell to the bottom of the lake where water insects shredded them into tiny pieces. Then fungi and bacteria digested the tiny pieces and released nutrients, which fed the algae growing on the tree. See how mossy it looks? Water insects and their larvae eat the bacteria and algae, and bluegills come to eat the insects on the tree. Then predators like great blue herons, largemouth bass and muskies come to feed on the bluegills."

"That really does sound like a hotel restaurant with a large buffet," Tessa said, delighted.

"Yeah, one that's open twenty-four hours a day," Hugo added.

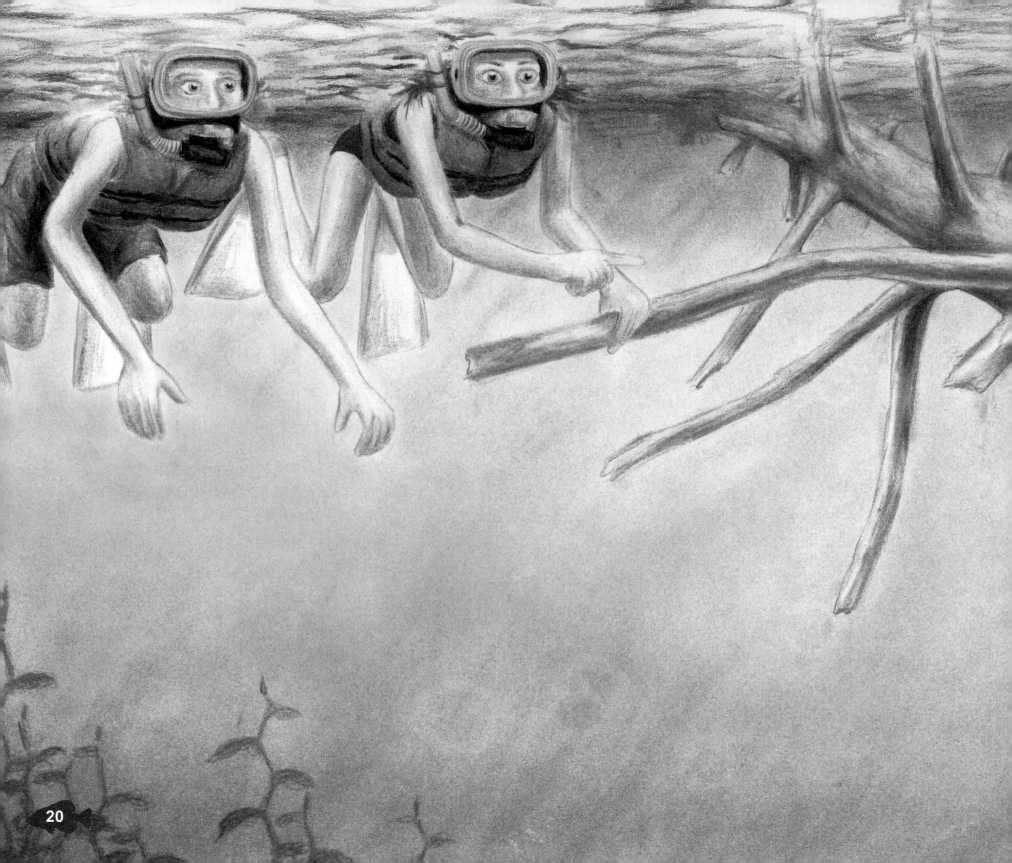

The kids went back underwater, and a bluegill swam down from the surface. All of a sudden, something big came speeding after it. The bluegill darted under the tree trunk just in time.

Both of the kids popped up. "It's a loon!" cried Hugo.

"Yes, they eat fish, too. Loons live on lakes with lots of fish and clear water so they can see the fish they eat for lunch," explained Carol.

Tessa looked around and noticed other trees nearby. "Did all of these trees fall into the lake, too?" she asked.

"Many did. When you have lots of trees growing along the shoreline, some fall in the water every few years and become new fish hotels. Last year, a friend of mine who studies fish helped me make a bigger fish hotel by adding a few more trees in the water. He cut the trees in the winter from that hill by the road and laid them on top of the ice. Then when the ice melted, they sank right where we wanted them.

The group of trees we have in the water now are home to many animals. It also protects my shoreline from waves, so it doesn't get washed into the lake. But the best part is that now some of my neighbors are also leaving their fallen trees in the lake."

The dinner bell rang. While eating, Hugo and Tessa told Uncle Henry all about the different fish they'd seen during their snorkeling adventure, and when they were done, the three of them walked down to the lake together. Uncle Henry said, "This afternoon I'm going to clean up the yard and chop up that poplar tree that fell in the water over there."

"No!" the kids cried.

"Uncle Henry, the little fish need that tree," Tessa explained. "It's their home; it keeps them safe from the big fish. This morning we watched them, and the largemouth bass would have eaten the little fish for sure if they didn't have the tree to hide in."

"Lots of other animals find homes in trees in the lake too," added Hugo.

"But that tree will get in the way of boaters," said Uncle Henry.

While Hugo, Tessa, and Uncle Henry were looking at the poplar tree and deciding what to do, they noticed a fisherman stop at the poplar tree to try his luck. Hugo pointed down the shoreline and said, "Uncle Henry, our neighbor Carol left the fallen trees on her shoreline to be a fish hotel. See it right there?"

After a long pause, Uncle Henry said, "Well, OK. I'll leave the tree in the water, then. People seem to like fishing there. And I guess the neighbors don't mind. I never thought about how leaving trees in the water helped fish; and I do want fish in our lake."

"Could we plant some trees near the water so there will be big underwater hotels for lots of animals to use when we're grown up?" asked Tessa.

Uncle Henry smiled and tousled her hair. "Sure," he said.

20 years later…

29

Glossary

- **Aquatic plant** – A plant that grows in water. Aquatic plants provide food and shelter for fish, wildlife, and the aquatic insects that in turn provide food for other organisms. Plants improve water quality, protect shorelines and lake bottoms,add to the aesthetic quality of the lake and impact recreation.

- **Aquatic insects** – Insects that live in the water during at least part of their lives. Aquatic insects are important in many ways, providing food for fish and serving as monitors for water quality. Page 10 shows a mayfly (upper left) and a water scorpion (center). Page 18 shows a caddisfly larva wrapped in pine needles, scuds (white) and a clubtail dragonfly (lower right).

- **Bluegills** – The most common sunfish in Wisconsin. Bluegills prefer warm, quiet waters and hide in the cover of weed beds. They can be found in small groups with other sunfish.

- **Crappie** – Crappies are found in open water and places with submerged stumps and logs, rocks and rocky ledges, deep pools in rivers, and areas with some aquatic vegetation reaching above the surface of the water. Black crappies are shown on page 9. Crappies travel and feed in loose schools, eating small aquatic organisms called "zooplankton" and aquatic insects and their larvae by filtering the food through their gill rakers (comblike structures in the gills). Older fish eat mostly minnows, immature bass, sunfish and perch.

- **Common Loon** – Expert divers, feeding on fish and aquatic invertebrates. Loons need clean, clear water because they search for fish by peering underwater from the surface. They nest along the water's edge and rear one or two chicks each summer. To help loons, protect natural shorelines, essential for suitable nesting habitat; minimize or eliminate fertilizers and erosion; and use lead-free fishing tackle like bismuth sinkers to reduce fatal lead poisoning. For more information see Loonwatch *www.northland.edu/sigurd-olson-environmental-institute-loon-watch.htm* and UW-Extension impervious surface publications and video *www.uwsp.edu/cnr-ap/clue/Pages/publications-resources/water.aspx*

- **Habitat** – The place where an animal lives that provides food, water, cover and space.

- **Largemouth Bass** – They don't call them "Bucketmouth" for nothing! The largest member of the sunfish family. Largemouth bass prefer warm water and like to hide under lily pads, docks, or in weed beds. They are eliminated from streams when the land draining to the stream is covered with too much hard (impervious) surfaces like rooftops, driveways and roads. See UW-Extension impervious surfaces publications and video *www.uwsp.edu/cnr-ap/clue/Pages/publications-resources/water.aspx*

- **Minnows** – Minnows serve as vital food sources for game fish such as walleye, smallmouth bass, and northern pike. A diverse community of minnows reduces the potential of adult game fish eating juvenile game fish. Wisconsin lakes are home to two groups of minnows. Mixed minnows (Cyprinidae) are seen swimming together in a shoal off the bottom of a lake. Minnows seen on the bottom of a lake are either juvenile gamefish or darters (Percidae, related to walleye and perch). Page 10 from left to right shows a blacknose shiner, two bluntnose minnows and a golden shiner.

An Iowa darter is shown on page 12 with the rock bass. Some minnows eat mixed vegetation (aquatic plants, phytoplankton and filamentous algae) and aquatic insects, and other minnows eat only aquatic insects.

- **Musky** (Muskellunge) – The largest predator fish in the state. Look for wide, vertical markings to distinguish musky from northern pike. Musky live alone, searching weed beds and tangles of old logs for prey. Shown on page 17.

- **Poplar** – Tree found over the entire state, but prefers sandy or rich soils that are moist such as lakeshores and wetlands. Sometimes confused with birch trees. The bark on poplar trees does not peel, whereas papery white birch bark does. Also known as popple or bigtooth aspen.

- **Rock Bass** – These bronze-colored panfish have large red eyes. Rock bass are known as "goggle-eyes" in some states. Rock bass like rocks! They can be found in rocky-bottomed lakes and rivers. Shown on page 13.

- **Snorkel** – A short, curved tube for a swimmer to breathe through while keeping the face under water.

- **White Pine** – Grows statewide in Wisconsin in sandy, well-drained soils and along rock ridges and can grow to be 100 feet tall. The soft bluish-green needles are 3-5 inches long and grow in bundles of five. You can remember that the white pine has five needles per bundle by counting the number of letters in the word white. 'White' has five letters; white pines have five needles per bundle. Fourteen species of fish were found in one submerged white pine in Katherine Lake, Wisconsin. See *A Second Life for Trees in the Lakes: As Useful in Water as They Were on Land* by Michael A. Bozek

Resources

- Bozek, Michael. 2001. A Second Life for Trees in Lakes: As Useful in Water as They Were on Land. Lakeline 21 (2001): 26-30.

- Bozek, Michael. 2015. A Second Life for Trees in Lakes: As Useful in Water as They Were on Land. University of Wisconsin Extension and Wisconsin Department of Natural Resources. *www.uwsp.edu/cnr-ap/clue/Documents/Water/TreesShoreline.pdf*

- Brickman, Robin, and Wendy Pfeffer. 1997. *A Log's Life*. Simon & Schuster.

- Cole, Henry. 2007. *On Meadowview Street*. Greenwillow Books.

- Nelson, Darby. 2011. *For Love of Lakes*. Michigan State University Press.

- Wisconsin Fish Sticks program *dnr.wi.gov/topic/fishing/outreach/fishsticks.html* Contact person: Scott Toshner, Fisheries Biologist, (715) 372-8539 Ext. 121 or Scott.Toshner@wisconsin.gov

- Wolter, Max. 2012. Lakeshore Woody Habitat in Review. Wisconsin Department of Natural Resources. *dnr.wi.gov/topic/fishing/documents/outreach/ LitWoodyHabReviewWolter2012.pdf*